PRAYING
A Book for Children

NANCY L. ROTH

Illustrated by Hondi Brasco

 CHURCH

Church Publishing Incorporated

NEW YORK

OTHER CHURCH PUBLISHING BOOKS BY
NANCY L. ROTH:

We Sing of God: a Hymnal for Children.
Robert N. Roth and Nancy L. Roth, Editors. 1989.

A Closer Walk: Meditating on Hymns for Year A. 1998.

Church Publishing Incorporated
445 Fifth Avenue
New York, N.Y. 10016

10 9 8 7 6 5

Acknowledgments

My thanks are due to Elizabeth Darlington, Nannette and Richard Fatigate, Ann Gordon, the Rev. Anita Schell-Lambert, and my husband Robert Roth, who read this manuscript and provided many helpful suggestions; to my illustrator, Hondi Brasco, whose understanding both of spirituality and of children has contributed so much to this book; and to my editor, Ray Glover, with whom, as always, it has been a pleasure to work.

For our young friends Kate and Emily Brasco
and Davidas Marathe
and our own grown children Christopher and Michael,
who have kept me in touch with childhood over the
years.

Contents

1

What Is Praying?

This book is for you, the young people who will be holding our earth's future in your hands. Some of you will read this book yourselves. Some of you will hear this book read to you by teachers, parents, grandparents, or your older brothers or sisters.

This book is about a very important subject: your friendship with God. It is about *praying*. What is praying? When I was your age, I learned in Sunday School that "praying is *talking* with God." When I grew up, I discovered that praying is much more than that. Praying includes *all* the ways that we grow in our friendship with God, not just the talking ways. Can you imagine talking non-stop to a friend? Don't you think your friend would get pretty tired of it? Talking with God is part of our praying, but it isn't the only part. After all, talking is not the only thing we do with our friends!

The better you know your friends, for example, the more

likely you are to *think* about them—even when you are not
actually together. "Hmmm, I wonder what Mary is doing on this rainy day. I wonder whether Chris's baseball
team is doing well in the game today. Why do you suppose
Ann seemed sad at recess? Wasn't Michael wonderful
in the school play!" Thinking about our friends is a part of
friendship.

Another way to enjoy friendship is to *work* with our
friends. It's fun to work on a class project in school, or to
plant a garden in a vacant lot with your friends, or to work
together on a recycling program in your neighborhood.
You get to know friends better when you work beside them.

The better you know someone, the more you are able to
listen to them, rather than fill up all the time with your own
talking. Then you really *notice* what *they* are thinking and
what *they* are feeling. Sometimes you can just sit together
silently, maybe on the front steps of your house or apart-
ment on a hot summer day, watching the fleecy clouds in
the sky and listening to the birds in the trees or the sounds
of the busy city, depending on where you live.

There are *many* ways we can grow closer to our friends, you see. Talking to them is only one of them. Some of the other ways are: thinking about them, working with them, listening to them, or just sitting silently beside them.

The more I've thought about it, the more all of this is true also of our friendship with God. We can, of course, talk to God. But we can also think about God. We can do God's work. We can just be silent and remember that God is with us. All of these ways of growing closer to God are ways of *praying.*

This book will give you many ideas about growing closer to God. *Noticing things*—like nature, other people, your feelings, and God's presence with you—helps you grow closer to God. *Thinking about God, working, playing, learning,* and even *deciding things* are other ways of praying. You will read about *"talking"* prayer only in the very last pages.

I hope that you will enjoy this book, because nothing is more *full of joy* than God's friendship, the friendship that is always there for you, forever.

Your Own Prayer Notebook

You will probably want to have a notebook with blank pages in which to write or draw some of the ideas which you will have while you read this book. With a spiral notebook you can tear out pages if you change your mind about something. Or you could buy a three-ring notebook and both lined paper for writing and unlined paper for drawing. As you read, you will find suggestions for lists or drawings which you can put in your notebook. This will be your *own* "prayer book" in which you write your thoughts and prayers. Some people call this a "journal." The word comes from the French word for "day," which is *jour*. Some people actually do write in their journals every day, and some people just write in them whenever they feel like it. Because it is your own prayer notebook or journal, you can use it exactly the way *you* want to!

2
Praying by Noticing

ne of the simplest kinds of praying is one you might call "the prayer of noticing." In this kind of praying, you become aware that God is with you and you are with God by noticing certain things. This is a kind of praying which you may do already—only you probably haven't known it was praying!

Noticing Nature

For example, have you ever noticed something beautiful outdoors? Noticing something wonderful in nature helps you become aware of God, who is the Creator. We call God the "Creator" because God made the whole Creation, which is another word for "the things that have been made." In the words of a favorite hymn ("All things bright and beautiful"), "The Lord God made them all!" Maybe one day you happened to lean down very close to a tulip and look inside. Wow! Or noticed some green grass pushing up through a tiny crack in a sidewalk. Amazing! Or maybe you touched a cool patch of soft green moss in the woods or the park, or felt the soft fur of your pet dog or cat. Have you noticed the rainbow colors shining from a pigeon's feathers? Did you ever wake up early enough to hear the birds' "dawn chorus," a kind of morning concert in which everybody—robins, bluejays, cardinals, thrushes, finches, and sparrows—sings at once? Have you ever watched a group of ants working together?

What about the sky? Whether you live in the city or the country, watching the sky change throughout the day can be like going to an art show. In some places, you can see big patches of sky. In other places, maybe you can see a small patch of sky, in an interesting shape between tall buildings. But wherever you see it, the sky is full of surprises. Sometimes, at sunrise or sunset, it turns rosy-orange. In the middle of the day, it might be bright blue, or blue with floating fleecy clouds, or plain grey. At night it is dark blue, almost black, and sometimes you can see the moon and the stars.

Have you noticed how the cool rain makes you feel more comfortable on a hot day? Have you enjoyed watching snowflakes fall from the sky and watching them land on your sleeve? Have you felt the warm sun shining on your face?

Some of the things that help us notice God's presence are very big, like the sky. And some are very small, like the tiny ants who seem to know exactly where they are going. Can you make your own list of things in nature that help you notice God? You can either write them down or draw them.

Noticing Human Beings

Of course, the creation includes the human beings God made too! We can pray by remembering that all people are God's children. God's creation includes people who are young and old, rich and poor, of every race and religion and country in the world. One of the ways to notice God through human beings is to *enjoy* all the different kinds of people there are and to remember that everyone is part of God's family. That is especially important to remember when we see people who are in need or in trouble or sick. Jesus said once, "When you do something for people who need help, you are doing it for me." By noticing people— really noticing them—we are noticing God's presence.

One time we can easily notice God's presence is when we are surrounded by the love of our families, friends, or teachers. When we feel happy and protected by the people who

love us, their love can help us notice *God's* love. When other people help us to learn and to grow, we can remember that learning and growing are what God wants for us too. But it is important to realize that even when we don't feel particularly loved by *people, God's* love is always with us.

Who are some of the human beings who help you notice God?

Noticing Feelings

When do you feel happy and peaceful? Is it when you are riding your bike, or when you are playing with your friends? Is it when you are curled up in an armchair reading one of your favorite books, or when your family has a special celebration, with good food and lots of relatives around? At times like these, life feels just right. When we feel happy or peaceful, it is easy to notice God.

But it is also true that we can notice God when we are *not* happy. Sometimes that is the only reason we can keep going! When we are lonely, God is with us as a friend. When we are afraid, God is with us as a protector. When we are angry, God is with us, understanding how we feel. When we are sick, God is with us helping us to get well. When we are sad, God is with us, comforting us. When we feel sorry about something we have done wrong, God is with us, forgiving us.

What are some of the feelings you have? Can you draw what they feel like?

Noticing God Through Quiet Listening

We can also pray by noticing God's presence through *quiet listening.* In quiet listening, noticing God is *all* you do! You do that by becoming very still, inside and outside. First, find a place where no one will bother you—maybe a special place in your backyard or in a park, a quiet church, or your bedroom with the door closed.

Then relax. You can relax by *shaking* the tenseness out of the legs, the arms, and the whole body. Or you can first tense each muscle of the body and then relax it.

Find a position in which you can be comfortable. Some people sit in a chair, some sit on the floor or the ground, and some people even lie down.

You can either close your eyes or leave your eyes partly open, but don't really look at anything.

Notice your breath. Try to breathe through your nose, not your mouth. Do you feel your breath going in and out, in and out?

Now, as you breathe, think of God being with you. If you want to, you can even "think" the word "God" or "Jesus" as you breathe, to help you notice God.

Do this for a few minutes. You will probably find that other thoughts sometimes take your mind far away. Don't worry about that. It happens to everybody! Just gently notice your breathing again and bring your mind back to God. As you practice, it will get easier.

This is a very simple way of praying, but many people say it is one of the most helpful ways. Praying by just noticing God's presence is like being with our best friend—any time we want!

3

Praying by Thinking About God

Just as using our minds and imaginations in thinking about our friends can help us know them better, *thinking* about God can help us to know God better. One of the ways we can pray in this way is to think about a Bible story. Do you think I'm talking only about sitting quietly, thinking? Of course, that's one way of thinking about God. But did you ever realize how many other *different* ways you can "think"?

Let's imagine, for example, that you have chosen to "think about" the story about Jesus in the Gospel of Mark, Chapter 4:

> On that day, when evening had come, Jesus said to his friends, "Let us go across to the other side of the lake." And leaving the crowd behind, they took him with them in the boat, just as he was. And other boats were with him.

And a great storm of wind arose, and the waves beat into the boat, so that the boat was already filling. But Jesus was in the back of the boat, asleep on the cushion; and they woke him up and said to him, "Teacher, do you not care if we die?"

He woke up and rebuked the wind, and said to the sea, "Peace! Be still!" Then the wind ceased, and there was a great calm.

He said to them, "Why are you afraid? Have you no faith?" And they were filled with awe, and said to one another, "Who then is this, that even wind and sea obey him?"

Thinking by Drawing

One of the ways you can think about this story is to draw it on paper. Can you draw the way water looks when there is a storm: big splashing waves? How would the sky look? Dark and cloudy? With rain coming down? Can you draw a small boat in the middle of that picture? Or maybe you'd like to cut out a boat from another piece of paper which can move up and down on the wavy water. How would *you* like to be in that small boat?

To think about the *whole* story, you have to draw *another* picture. This one will be a picture of how everything looked *after* Jesus said, "Peace! Be still!" The lake will be calm—

gentle wavy lines or maybe even straight lines. The sky will be blue again. Maybe the sun will be out. Your boat will move very differently in this picture. *Now* would you like to be in the boat?

Thinking by Moving

Another way you can think about the story is to act it out through movement. You could *be* the water, for example. If you have a blue or green scarf to wave, so much the better. At first, you can be the calm water, and then you can let the storm happen. Move your arms and body up and down with energy! Then imagine that you hear Jesus saying "Peace! Be still!" and make your movements calm again.

Or you could imagine that you are Jesus' friends. Huddle down low as if you were frightened. You would probably shiver from fear as well as from the cold water splashing over the boat. How would you act when Jesus stops the storm? Would you straighten up your body and breathe a big sigh of relief?

Thinking by Making Music

You can think about God by making music. For example, make up your own sounds and music for this story. You can do it with your voice, or you can use instruments or other objects which make the sounds you want. Can you make the sound of the water with your voice? "shhhh. . . . ssshhhSSSHHHssshhh. . . . ssshhhSSSHHHssshhh. . . ." getting louder and louder and faster and faster. Can you make the sound of thunder? "BOOOOOOOMMMMM." (Your mother may let you borrow a big pot lid which can help make the storm sounds.) The sound of the boat creaking? "Creeeeekkkk." The cries of Jesus' friends: "HELP!" How would Jesus' voice sound? "Peace! Be still!" How would the water sound then? "SSSHHH. . . . ssshhh. . . . sshh. . . ."

You might make up a song of your own about the story.

You could tell the story in your own words to a tune you make up as you go along. On the other hand, you could do a lot of planning. You could choose a tune which you like, and then write down your own words for the song. Maybe a grown-up will help you write it down with the notes.

You could sing a hymn that has some of the ideas in the story. There is a hymn, for example, that is sometimes called the "Navy Hymn." It asks for God's protection for sailors on the sea.

> *Almighty Father, strong to save,*
> *whose arm hath bound the restless wave,*
> *who bidd'st the mighty ocean deep*
> *its own appointed limits keep:*
> *O hear us when we cry to thee*
> *for those in peril on the sea.*
>
> (Hymn 579, *The Hymnal 1982:* New York,
> The Church Hymnal Corporation)

When you have learned this hymn, it is fun to sway back and forth with the melody as if you were on a boat.

There is a hymn from the Dakota Indian tribe, "Many and great," which is fun to sing with a drum. If you do not have a drum, there are other things you can use as a drum, such as oatmeal boxes, yogurt containers, even pots and pans.

Many and great, O God, are thy works,
maker of earth and sky;
thy hands have set the heavens with stars;
thy fingers spread the mountains and plains:
Lo, at thy word the waters were formed;
'deep seas obey thy voice.

(Hymn 385, *The Hymnal 1982:* New York,
The Church Hymnal Corporation.)

Do you think that Jesus' friends in the boat realized that Jesus had God's power, since the "deep seas obeyed his voice"?

I have discovered that all of these ways of using our imagination—drawing, moving or acting, and singing and making music—are a way of praying because they help us all to understand more about God. They are a way of asking a question. The question is: "What does this Bible story say to *me*, someone who lives many years after the story happened?"

When you have felt the movement of a stormy lake become calm through acting it out, you can also feel how God brings peace into other kinds of storms, like hurt or angry feelings.

When you realize what happened when Jesus' friends asked him for help, it can remind you that *you* can ask for help from God—*any time!*

Here is a list of a few of my favorite stories to "think about" in these ways, to get you started. Beside each story is the place you can find it in the part of the Bible called the "New Testament." You can also find these stories in a Children's Bible. They tell about some of the ways people from long ago knew that God was their friend. Some of them are called "parables," stories that Jesus himself told to help people understand God better.

Using your mind and imagination will help you understand all of these stories better. You will get new ideas about your own friendship with God. So, even though you may use no words at all, thinking is an important way of praying.

The Wedding at Cana (John 2:1-11)
The Miraculous Catch of Fish (Luke 5:1-11)

The Healing of the Paralyzed Man (Mark 2:1-12)
The Parable of the Sower (Mark 4:1-9)
The Parable of the Mustard Seed (Mark 4:30-32)
The Feeding of the Five Thousand (Mark 6:30-44)
Jesus Walking on the Water (Matt. 14:22-33)
The Parable of the Good Samaritan (Luke 10:29-37)
The Parable of the Prodigal Son (Luke 15:11-32)
Mary and Martha (Luke 10:38-42)
The Healing of Ten Lepers (Luke 17:11-19)
The Healing of Bartimaeus (Mark 10:46-52)
Zacchaeus (Luke 19:1-10)
The Good Shepherd (John 10:11-15)
Gethsemane (Mark 14:32-42)
The Crucifixion (Luke 23:33-46)
The Resurrection (Mark 16:1-8)

4

Praying In Work and In Play

Working Along With God

You have probably already discovered that friendship with God can grow when you do kind or useful things. That is because God loves the world and wants it to be a happy and healthy place. Can you think of some of the things you do which help your friendship with God grow? Maybe you help rake leaves or sweep the sidewalk, clean a room, or pick up garbage. Maybe you help carry groceries, plant a garden, or water the houseplants. Maybe you send a get-well card to someone who is in the hospital. Or visit a neighbor who is handicapped, old, or ill and unable to get out. You might even offer to shop for them! Maybe you help collect clothes or food for people who need them, or even share your own clothes, toys, and food with others. You might enter a "walkathon" to raise money for a good cause. Maybe you help recycle bottles or newspapers. There are many, many ways to work along with God. Working along with God is like praying with your *hands*. Can you write or draw some of the ways you can think of to work along with God?

Making and Doing Things

Some artists say that when they draw or paint or make a sculpture, it feels like praying. It makes them feel happy and free. Musicians have said the same thing about composing music, playing an instrument, or singing. Dancers have said the same thing about dancing.

These kinds of praying are not only for people who make a living doing these things, but for everybody who likes to do them. That is because God gives us each "gifts." They are not the kind of gifts you unwrap when you have a birthday. They are the gifts of being *able* to do certain things. For example, do you like to swim or play basketball or other sports? Do you like to act in plays, or to help take care of younger children? Do you like to write stories or draw pictures, to fix things or to build things? Do you like to sing, play an instrument, or dance? These are some of your gifts. We all have gifts, and God, the Creator, loves to see us use them. When we use them, we are using God's gifts to *us*. These gifts make us feel happy and free. They make other people happy when we use them.

Another thing about gifts is that we don't all have every gift! For example, I never was good at sports like softball.

When I would try to play with my brothers, I'd always strike out, and I never was able to catch the ball very well. In fact, one time I let it crash into my nose! One thing that made me feel better was that I *was* good at playing the piano. You may wish you were good in sports, but you are not. Instead, you are probably good at something else.

Some people's eyes are good at seeing softballs, but they can't play an instrument like the piano or guitar. Some people's eyes are good at reading music, but they have a hard time seeing softballs, tennis balls, or even large basketballs coming towards them. Some people's bodies are strong, and they can lift heavy things, but they are not very flexible. Some people's bodies are flexible, and they can bend easily, but they are not as strong. Some people's imaginations think in pictures, and they can draw very well, but they have trouble writing things down. Some people's imaginations think in words, and they can write wonderful stories, but they have trouble drawing things. Some people's minds are good at remembering numbers, but they have trouble re-membering the faces of people they have met just a few weeks before. Some people's minds are good at remembering people's faces, but they have trouble remembering their own telephone number!

It doesn't mean that we shouldn't *try* everything that we want to: playing softball, playing the piano, lifting, bending, drawing, writing, remembering numbers *and* faces. It is just that we do not need to feel bad if some things are harder for us than other things.

What are some things that are hard for you? What are some things that are easy for you? What are some of the things that make you feel happy and free? What are some of your gifts?

Learning

Did you know that *learning things* can be praying? When you think about it, your mind is one of the most important gifts God has given you. Your mind is filled with curiosity about many things. When you take the time to follow that curiosity and to learn about the world around you, you probably appreciate God's world more. So, even if going to school or doing your homework doesn't always *seem* like growing in friendship with God, it can be! You can learn in other ways as well, like going to museums, watching certain "specials" on public TV, taking lessons in some subject, or reading books from the library. Learning about God's interesting world makes life more fun and helps you become a more interesting human being too.

Deciding Things

Sometimes we have to decide whether or not to do something.

Maybe some of our friends want us to join them in doing something we don't think is right, like stealing someone's Halloween jack o'lantern and smashing it on the street.

Maybe the whole class has ganged up against a new student who has a different way of dressing and talking. If you are kind to that person, the rest of the class will make fun of you. But you know that all people are loved by God, and you do not want to join in your friends' teasing.

Maybe you go to a picnic at the playground where everybody leaves junk all over the place and you are the only one to throw yours in the trash.

Maybe there is a grown-up in your neighborhood or someone on TV whose example you *think* it might be smart to follow. It might be somebody selling drugs or somebody who just fights with everyone instead of trying to solve problems by talking about them. But you decide not to follow those examples, because you know down deep that harming others is not the way God wants you to live.

Maybe you know that some things are not good for your body, like sitting around watching TV all day long or eating a lot of junk food. You may see older friends smoking cigarettes or taking drugs, and you wonder if life would be more fun if you did those things too. But you know down deep that the best way to have fun is to take care of the body that God gave you so that you can really be healthy and alive, not just partly alive! So you decide to take good care of your body.

Maybe it would be much easier to put off doing your homework or other jobs. Not doing them seems like the easiest thing to do. But you know down deep that the home-work or those jobs won't go away, and you probably wouldn't feel any more like doing them later. You decide to do what needs to be done because you know that, once the jobs are done, there will be plenty of time to play.

It is very difficult to choose what you know is right for you, rather than what is easiest to do. It is very difficult when you find you have to decide not to go along with other people. But a very important way to grow in friendship with God is to decide to do what is right, even if it is hard, *and* to do it without acting as if you were better than everybody else.

Doing what *you* believe is right rather than just going along with other people is a very important way of praying.

Playing

The words "praying" and "playing" are just alike except for one letter. When we take time to rest and to play and enjoy life, we are, in a way, saying "thank you" to our Creator. Young people are probably better at this kind of praying than adults. Praying by playing can be as simple as playing ball, swinging high on a swing, or getting together with friends to dance to your favorite music. It can even be just sitting in the sun on a nice day, enjoying life!

Playing helps us to feel more like the human beings we are meant to be—happy and healthy. Playing helps us to enjoy God's greatest gift to us: our life!

5
Praying With Words

As we said at the beginning, most people think of *talking* when they think of praying. But "talking prayer" is not just saying some words: it is *sharing all your thoughts with God.* When you talk with your best friends, you probably find that you can be very honest. You share with them the things that make you angry or sad, as well as the things that make you happy. The same is true with God. You can, in fact, tell God everything!

Prayers from the Bible

There are prayers from the Bible that help you think of the things you want to tell God. These prayers were originally prayed in the languages of Hebrew, Aramaic, and Greek, which were the languages of the people who wrote the Bible. The prayers we use from the Bible are translations

into the English language, and different people have trans-
lated them in different ways. For example, when Jesus'
friends asked him, "Lord, teach us to pray," he taught them
the prayer called the Lord's Prayer. You may know a trans-
lation of the Lord's Prayer that is different from the one in
this book, but it is the same prayer in the original language.
The Lord's Prayer has always been the favorite prayer of
Christians because it includes many things we want to share
with God. Let me show you what I mean.

*Our Father in heaven, hallowed be your Name, your kingdom
come, your will be done, on earth as in heaven.*
> These words mean that we believe that God is holy
> ("hallowed") and that we hope the earth will be the
> place God intended it to be, where people live in
> harmony and peace.

Give us today our daily bread.
> We ask God for the things we need in order to live,
> such as bread or enough food, because we know that
> God is the giver of all good things.

Forgive us our sins as we forgive those who sin against us.
> When we say these words, we tell God that we are
> sorry when we have hurt other people in any way,
> and we also say that we want to forgive other people
> who have hurt us.

Save us from the time of trial, and deliver us from evil.

We ask God's help in keeping us away from wanting to do bad things, and we ask God's protection from things that can hurt us.

For thine is the kingdom, and the power, and the glory, for ever and ever. Amen.

These words are about God's love, which is more powerful and glorious than anything else in the world—and which will last forever. The very last word in many prayers, "Amen," means "I want it to be this way" in the Hebrew language in which many of our prayers were first written.

There are other wonderful prayers in the Bible, such as Mary's prayer called "The Magnificat." Mary said this prayer after the Angel Gabriel told her she would be the mother of Jesus. You can find that prayer if you look in the Gospel of Luke in the first chapter, verses 46–55.

My soul magnifies the Lord,
and my spirit rejoices in God my Savior,
for he has regarded the low estate of his handmaiden.
For behold, henceforth all generations will call me blessed;
for he who is mighty has done great things for me,
and holy is his name.
And his mercy is on those who fear him
from generation to generation.
He has shown strength with his arm,
he has scattered the proud in the imagination of their hearts,
he has put down the mighty from their thrones,
and exalted those of low degree;
he has filled the hungry with good things,
and the rich he has sent empty away.
He has helped his servant Israel,
in remembrance of his mercy,
as he spoke to our fathers,
to Abraham and to his posterity for ever.

In this prayer, Mary says her soul "magnifies" the Lord. Have you ever looked through a magnifying glass and seen something that is usually almost invisible, like a grain of sand, seem very large? Magnifying glasses make things become *greater* or larger. Mary was so happy that she probably even *sang* this prayer about God's *greatness*. In a way, her prayer "magnified" God!

She also sang about how wonderful it was that God had chosen someone who was poor, or of "low estate," to be the mother of Jesus. God could have chosen a great princess or someone who was famous or powerful. It was as if the world were turned topsy-turvy! Instead of giving special gifts to the people who were proud and mighty and rich, God gave them to people who were humble and powerless and hungry. Mary remembered that God had promised her ancestor Abraham many years ago that God would always be merciful and help Abraham's descendents. And now she knew it was true.

And, of course, there is a whole prayer book in the Bible, called the Book of Psalms. The Psalms—150 of them—were written long before Jesus was born, so that they were Jesus' prayer book too. The Psalms were originally sung while an instrument called the "psaltery" was played. It had strings (no one is sure exactly how many) which were plucked, like a guitar or a harp. You may want to make your own "psaltery" by taking a strong box (like a cigar box or egg carton) and stretching several rubber bands over it for strings. "Tune" your psaltery by stretching or loosening the rubber bands so that they play the notes you want. Then try singing the Twenty-third Psalm to a tune you make up, while you pluck your psaltery. The Twenty-third Psalm is a favorite prayer about God's care for us.

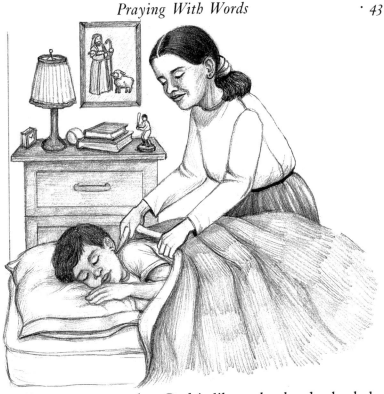

This prayer says that God is like a shepherd who helps his sheep find green grass to eat and fresh water to drink, guides them along the right paths, and protects them from danger. In fact, God loves us so much it is like having God give a party for us—spreading out food on a table and pouring so much into our drinking cup that it overflows. At the time the psalms were written, one of the things people did to welcome guests was to pour sweet perfumed oil on their heads, which was called "anointing" their heads with oil.

The Lord is my shepherd;
I shall not be in want.
He makes me lie down in green pastures
   and leads me beside still waters.
He revives my soul
   and guides me along right pathways for his Name's sake.
Though I walk through the valley of the shadow of death,
I shall fear no evil;
   for you are with me;
   your rod and your staff, they comfort me.
You spread a table before me in the presence of those
               who trouble me;
   you have anointed my head with oil,
   and my cup is running over.
Surely your goodness and mercy shall follow me all the days
            of my life,
   and I will dwell in the house of the Lord for ever.

There are other prayers which we say in church, such as the *Sanctus. Sanctus* is the Latin word for "holy," and that is just what it says:

> *Holy, holy, holy Lord, God of power and might,*
> *heaven and earth are full of your glory,*
> *Hosanna in the highest.*

If you want to see where that prayer came from, ask someone to help you find Isaiah 6:3 in the Bible. There you can read about the prophet Isaiah, who saw angels singing in the temple. When we say or sing the *Sanctus,* we are joining in the prayer of the angels. We add "Hosanna in the Highest", which is a way to ask God to be with us. *Hosanna* means "be our help" in the Hebrew language.

The *Sanctus* is usually followed by the *"Benedictus,"* which is simply the Latin way of saying "blessed:"

> *Blessed is he who comes in the name of the Lord.*
> *Hosanna in the highest.*

This prayer is found in the Bible too. Look in the New Testament for Matthew 21:9, where the people shout those words when Jesus enters the city of Jerusalem on Palm Sunday.

You see that many of our prayers were first said by people who worshipped God long ago. What other prayers do you often say in church?

Prayers from Prayer Books

Other prayers you say in church were written by people who lived since the Bible was written. For example, in some churches there is a beautiful prayer in a service called "Compline," which is a service for nighttime, just before going to bed. This prayer was first used long ago in monasteries, which were places where people gathered to live a life of worship and prayer. But it would be a wonderful prayer for *everybody* to say before going to sleep:

Guide us waking, O Lord, and guard us sleeping; that awake we may watch with Christ, and asleep we may rest in peace.

Another prayer in many prayer books is said to have been written by St. Francis of Assisi:

Lord, make us instruments of your peace.
Where there is hatred, let us sow love;
where there is injury, pardon;
where there is discord, union;
where there is doubt, faith;
where there is despair, hope;
where there is darkness, light;
where there is sadness, joy.
Grant that we may not so much seek to be consoled as to
    console;
to be understood as to understand;
to be loved as to love.
For it is in giving that we receive;
it is in pardoning that we are pardoned;
and it is in dying that we are born to eternal life. Amen.

That prayer is about the way of living shown by Jesus, which St. Francis followed too: a way of peace and love and giving rather than fighting, hating, and getting.

"Grace"

Maybe you have prayers you say regularly at home. Does your family say special prayers called "grace" at meals? The word "grace" comes from the Latin word for "thank you," so this prayer is a "thank you" prayer for our food and other blessings. Sometimes people hold hands around the table while they are saying "grace," and sometimes they fold their hands in their laps. A favorite "grace" is:

Bless, O God, this food to our use and us to your service, and make us ever mindful of the needs of others; through Jesus Christ our Lord. Amen.

Another "grace" is:

God is great,
God is good;
Let us thank God for this food. Amen.

A very old prayer for meal times is:

Blessed are you, O Lord God, Creator of the Universe, for you give us food to sustain our lives and make our hearts glad; through Jesus Christ our Lord. Amen.

This next one can also be sung, to a tune called "Old Hundredth:"

Praise God from whom all blessings flow;
Praise God all creatures here below;
Praise God above ye heavenly host;
Praise Father, Son, and Holy Ghost. Amen.

Making Up Your Own Prayers

So far, the "talking prayers" we have seen were made up by someone else. But you can make up your own prayers, too. You do that by telling God the things you have on your mind. It might be something like this:

O God, I love your world. Thank you for everything. Please take care of my family—my mom and dad and my sister and my dog Lucky. Help me to be kind and fair to my friends. Amen.

Or it might be:

God, I'm so mad. Jimmy got chosen to be captain of the team and I think I deserved it. Help me not to be mean to Jimmy. Amen.

Or:

God, I'm worried. My grandma is sick. I don't want her to die. Help me to understand you are always with her, and with me, too. Amen.

You can even write down your own prayers. Some people write their prayers as "letters to God." You could begin, "Dear God" and then tell God the things you have on your mind. Because God is your friend, you can tell God *every-thing* when you are praying.

6
Praying
All Day Long

Most people find that special times of praying, like grace at meals, or prayers at certain times of day, help them to remember God's friendship *all* day long.

When you wake up in the morning, you can thank God for the new day and ask God to help you in everything you do that day.

When you go to bed, you can think about your day and ask God to forgive you for any wrong things you wish you hadn't done. You can ask God to take care of people you care about. You may wish to keep a list of people who are sick or in need in your prayer notebook, so that you will remember them all. You can ask God for peace in the world. You can ask God to help you with any problems you have. You can thank God for all God's gifts or blessings—especially for life! Bedtime is a special time for talking with God, thinking about God, and quiet listening.

At special prayer times, some people like to kneel with

their head bowed and their hands folded. But that certainly is not the only way to pray! Some people prefer to pray standing up, with their arms stretched out, as if they were holding their prayers in their hands before God. Some people like to sit cross-legged on the floor with their hands on their knees. Some people like to pray sitting in a chair with their hands in their lap. You can find the position in which you feel best for praying. You can pray kneeling, sitting, standing, or lying down. You can pray walking, you can pray dancing, you can pray singing, you can pray working. I could go on and on.

Is it beginning to seem as if your entire life can be "praying?" That wouldn't be surprising, because it is true. You are very lucky if you can begin to understand this now, because many people don't understand it, even when they are quite old. They think that praying is only saying some words. But *you* know that praying is *everything* we do that helps us grow in friendship with God: talking, thinking, moving, deciding, working, making, playing—everything!

Amen.